Our Trip to the Firehouse

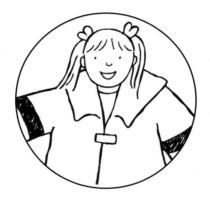

HOUGHTON MIFFLIN   BOSTON

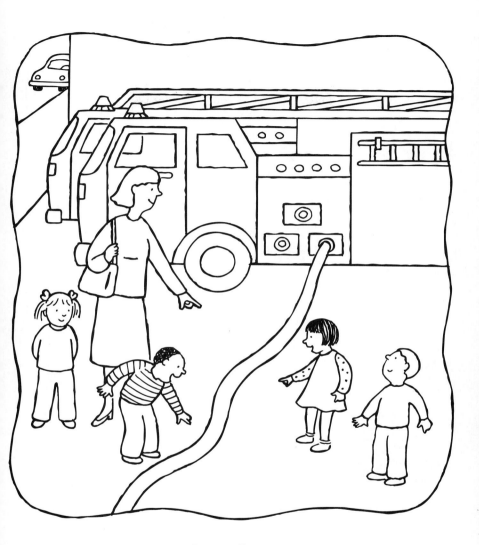

We're at the firehouse.
We see trucks and a
huge hose.

1

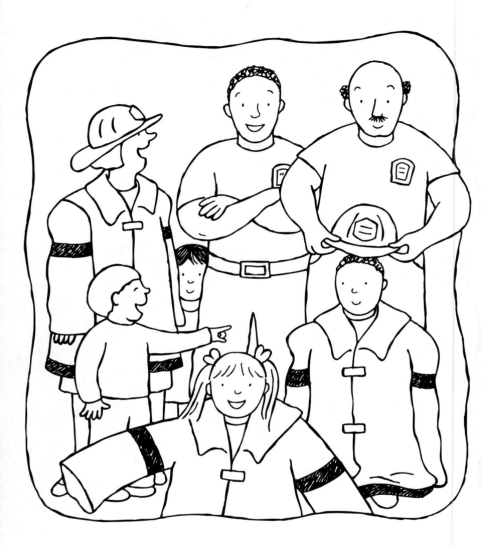

We meet the firefighters.
We put on their coats
and hats.

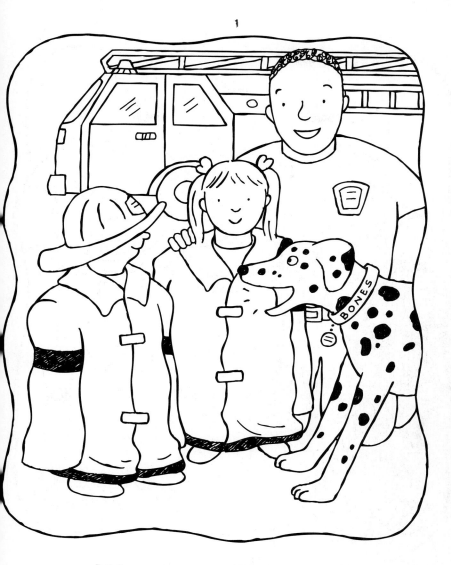

We meet Bones.
He barks at us.

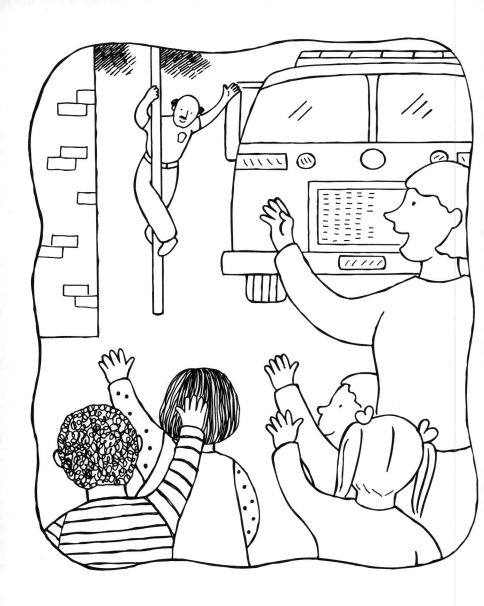

It's time to go.
Everyone waves good-bye.